BIG
FUN

Mario Herrera **Barbara Hojel**

Big Fun 1

Pearson Education, 10 Bank Street, White Plains, NY 10606 USA

Staff credits: The people who made up the *Big Fun* team, representing editorial, production, design, manufacturing, and marketing are Isabel Arnaud, Rhea Banker, Danielle Belfiore, Carol Brown, Kim Casey, Tracey Munz Cataldo, Dave Dickey, Gina DiLillo, Christine Edmonds, Erin Ferris, Nancy Flaggman, Yoko Mia Hirano, Penny Laporte, Christopher Leonowicz, Emily Lippincott, Maria Pia Marrella, Jennifer McAliney, Kate McLoughlin, Linda Moser, Kyoko Oinuma, Leslie Patterson, Sherri Pemberton, Salvador Pereira, Pamela Pia, Juan Carlos Portillo, Jennifer Raspiller, Aristeo Redondo, Nicole Santos, Susan Saslow, Kimberley Silver, Jane Townsend, Kenneth Volcjak, Lauren Weidenman, and Carmen Zavala.
Text composition: TSI Graphics
Illustration credits: Blanca Nayelli Barrera, Luis Briseño, Laura Estela González, Félix León, Hugo Miranda, Javier Montiel, A Corazón Abierto.
Photo credits: Page 1 (boy) Juerco Boerner/Glow Images, (crayon) Cara Purdy/Shutterstock;(puppet) Tania Zbrodko/Shutterstock; (paper) Irina Nartova/Shutterstock; (shelf) Andrea Crisante/ Shutterstock; p. 2 (top) Maria Pia Marrella/Pearson, (middle) Alex James Bramwell/Shutterstock, (bottom) Venus Angel/Shutterstock; p. 3 (top) Cara Purdy/Shutterstock, (middle) VectorShots.com/ Fotolia, (bottom) Photobac/Shutterstock; p. 10 (background) Joy Prescott/Fotolia, (left) Ionia/Shutterstock, (middle) hwongcc/Shutterstock, (right) irin-k/Shutterstock; p. 13 Design Pics Inc./Alamy; p. 14 (top) Stephanie Frey/Shutterstock, (middle) Stephanie Frey/Shutterstock, (bottom) Stephanie Frey/Shutterstock; p. 15 Harm Kruyshaar/Shutterstock; p. 22 (background) reggis382/Fotolia, (left) Daniel Prudek/Fotolia, (right) Pavel Timofeev/Fotolia; p. 23 Sergiy Bykhunenko/Shutterstock; p. 24 (left 3) Stephanie Frey/Shutterstock, (right 3) Harm Kruyshaar/Shutterstock; p. 25 Kyu Oh/Getty Images; p. 26 (top) Andrey Arkusha/Shutterstock, (middle) Kurhan/Fotolia, (bottom) Heather LaVelle/Shutterstock; p. 27 (top) Supri Suharjoto/Shutterstock, (middle) Kenishirotie/Fotolia, (bottom) bst2012/Fotolia; p. 34 (background) blickwinkel/Alamy, (left) Pat Thielen/Alamy, (bottom) Alison Thompson/Alamy; p. 35 Phase4Photography/Shutterstock; p. 37 (left) Oksana Kuzmina/Shutterstock, (middle left) mates/Fotolia, (middle right) Olgysha/Shutterstock, (right) mates/Fotolia; p. 38 (top) Cheuk-king Lo/Pearson Education Asia Ltd, (middle) mates/Fotolia, (bottom) Diana Taliun/Fotolia; p. 39 (top) fotos_v/Fotolia, (middle) Dave King/Dorling Kindersley, Ltd, (bottom) Second Story Images/Fotolia; p. 46 Roman Ponomarev/Fotolia, (bottom) vita khorzhevska/Shutterstock; p. 47 Andrey Arkusha/Shutterstock; p. 49 Vanessa Davies/DK Images, (cookie) Richard Villalon/Fotolia; p. 50 (top) Brent Hofacker/Fotolia, (middle) Odua Images/Fotolia, (bottom) Terry Leung/Pearson Education Asia Ltd; p. 51 (top) HandmadePictures/Fotolia, (middle) HomeStudio/Shutterstock, (bottom) Odua Images/Fotolia; p. 58 (left) Martin Sandberg/Getty Images, (bottom left) Anna Kucherova/Fotolia, (right) Michael Gray/Fotolia, (bottom right) HomeStudio/Shutterstock; p. 59 (left) Purestock/Alamy, (right) majesticca/Fotolia; p. 61 (left) sequarell/Fotolia, (right) Kevin/Fotolia; p. 62 (top) Irina Rogov/Shutterstock, (middle) maxstockphoto/Shutterstock, (bottom) Ruslan Kudrin/Shutterstock; p. 63 (top) Elnur/Shutterstock, (middle) Trevor Clifford/Pearson Education Ltd, (bottom) Karkas/ Shutterstock; p. 70 Dann Tardif/LWA/Corbis/Glow Images, (bottom left) Joseph Salonis/Fotolia, (bottom middle) Nature & Scenics/John Foxx Collection/Imagestate/Pearson; p. 71 Rob Marmion/ Shutterstock; p. 73 Margarita Borodina/Shutterstock, (top right) Oleksandr Dibrova/Fotolia, (top right) Azaliya (Elya Vatel)/Fotolia; p. 74 (top) haveseen/Fotolia, (middle) worker/Shutterstock, (bottom) Mi.Ti./Fotolia; p. 75 (top) Vincent/Fotolia, (middle) Miroslav Hlavko/Shutterstock, (bottom) Azaliya (Elya Vatel)/Fotolia; p. 82 (background) PHOTO FUN/Shutterstock, (left) sommai/Fotolia, (middle) whitaker/Shutterstock, (right) Michael Tieck/Fotolia; p. 83 Blend Images/Alamy;p. 85 (left) Paulaphoto /Shutterstock; (left) Gelpi JM/Shutterstock, (right) Comstock Images/Getty Images; p. 86 (top) gwimages/Fotolia, (middle) Hugh Sitton/age fotostock, (bottom) Michael Folmer/Alamy; p. 87 (top) Igor Mojzes/Fotolia, (middle) Goodluz/Shutterstock, (bottom) Yuri Arcurs/Shutterstock; p. 94 (left, middle, right) Emilia Stasiak/Shutterstock, (bottom left) kiya-nochka/Shutterstock, (bottom right) Frank Greenaway/Dorling Kindersley; p. 95 JGI/Jamie Grill/Getty Images; p. 97 Blend Images/SuperStock; p. 98 Zoroyan/Shutterstock; p. 99 serrnovik/Shutterstock.
Consultants and Reviewers: Leticia Aguilar Maldonado, Mexico City • Jocelyn Arcos Morales, Mexico City • Irma Canales Garrido, Mexico City • María Alejandra Escobedo Maciel, Mexico City • Laura García López, Mexico City • Marís Gómez Palestino, Escuela Mexicana Bilingüe, Mexico City • Rosa Lirio Cepeda Pérez, Institución Asunción de México, Mexico City • Choonje Lee, PLS Korea • Angel López, Colegio Monte Rosa, Mexico City • Wendy Paola Méndez Cruz, Mexico City • Araceli Mendoza Negrete, Mexico City • Fabiola Mora Gálvez, Universidad Motolinia, Mexico City • Georgina Mora Gálvez, Universidad Motolinia, Mexico City • Rocío Morales Romero, Mexico City • Leticia Aurora Moreno González, C.D.I.I. Melanie Kleine, Mexico City • Pedro Olmos Medina, Colegio Maestro Carlos Chávez, Mexico City • R. Norma Pérez Rodríguez, Mexico City • Karen Polanco, Colegio Monte Rosa, Mexico City • Helen Santoyo Orozco, Escuela Cristóbal Colón, Mexico City • María Guadalupe Torres Patiño, Escuela Cristóbal Colón, Mexico City
Music credits: Music composed by John Farrell, Hope River Music, www.johnfarrell.net, and Jeff Miller, Grant's Corners, Walden, NY, assisted by Conway Chewning. Music and vocal recordings produced by Jeff Miller and John Farrell. Recorded and mixed by Jeff Miller at Grant's Corners, Remote Recordings, Yorktown Heights, NY, and Hillsdale, NY.
Song lyrics by Barbara Hojel, with contributions by John Farrell. Children's vocal performance directed by Lorraine Cich. Child vocal performers: Julia Apostolou, Aisha Bhakta, Emma Halderman, Cassidy Kenney, Juliana Moscati; adult vocal performers: Lorraine Cich, John Farrell, Maggie Farrell, Ann Marie Lord.
Edit: Eastern Sky Media Services, Inc. Casselberry, Florida. Produced by Jon W. Reames and David E. Brown.
Recording and Audio Production Services: CityVox, LLC, 630 9th Ave. Suite 415 New York, NY 10036.

Printed in China
ISBN-10: 0-13-294054-X
ISBN-13: 978-0-13-294054-2
13 17

PEARSON ELT ON THE WEB

PearsonELT.com offers a wide range of classroom resources and professional development materials. Access course-specific websites, product information, and Pearson offices around the world.

Visit us at **www.pearsonELT.com**.

CONTENTS

Press-outs and Stickers included!

Chorus

BIG FUN
Song

Chorus

From the sky to the ground
And all the way around—
We can have big fun!
If there's rain, if there's sun,
Let's play with everyone.
We can have big, big fun!

Take a walk outside.
Our world is big and wide.
There are flowers and trees
And yellow bumblebees.
Buzz, buzz, buzz!

(Chorus)

Join your hands with me.
Let's see what we can see!
Then take a closer look.
We'll learn beyond our book.
Look, oh, look!

(Chorus)

① MY CLASS

1 Look and predict. Listen.

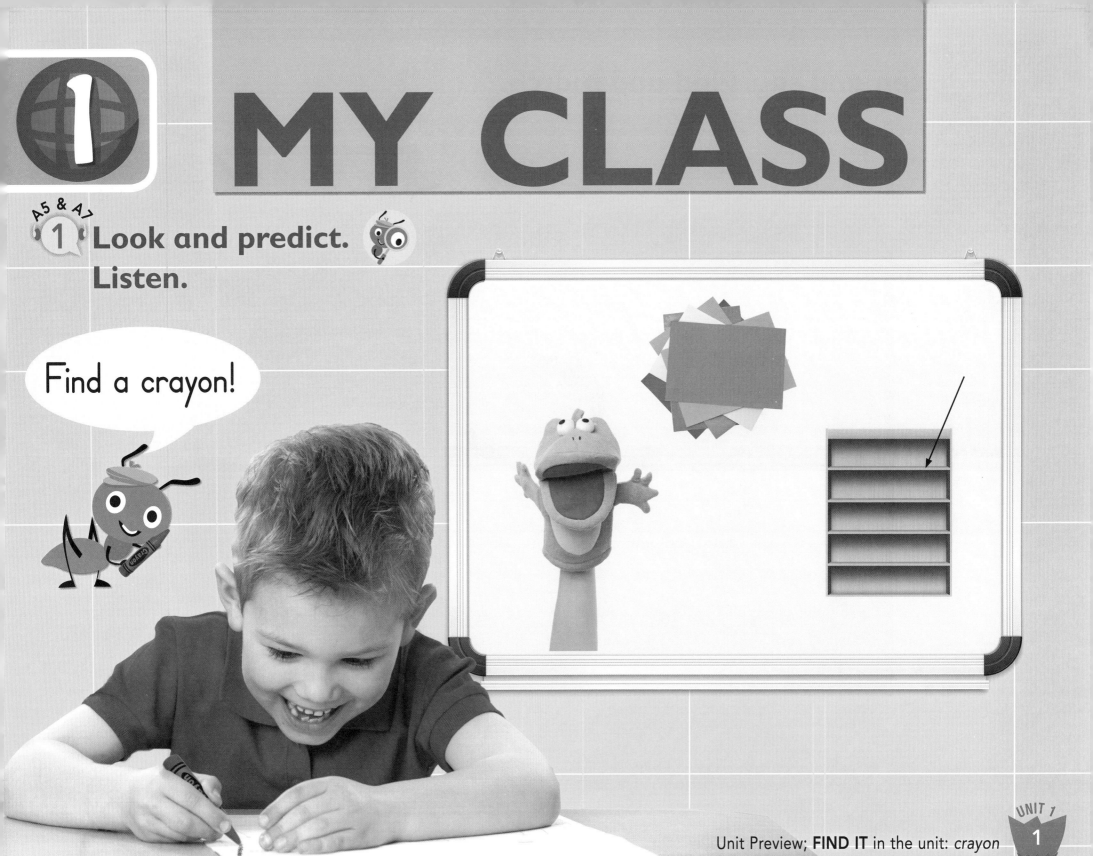

Unit Preview; **FIND IT** in the unit: *crayon*

2 Listen and say. Find and match.

Vocabulary Presentation: *puppet, chair, table*
Language Presentation: *What is this? It is (a puppet).*

3 Listen and say. Find and match.

Vocabulary Presentation: *crayon, paper, shelf*; Vocabulary Practice: *puppet, table, chair*
Language Practice: *What is this? It is (a crayon).*

4 **Paste press-outs and say.**

This is a table!

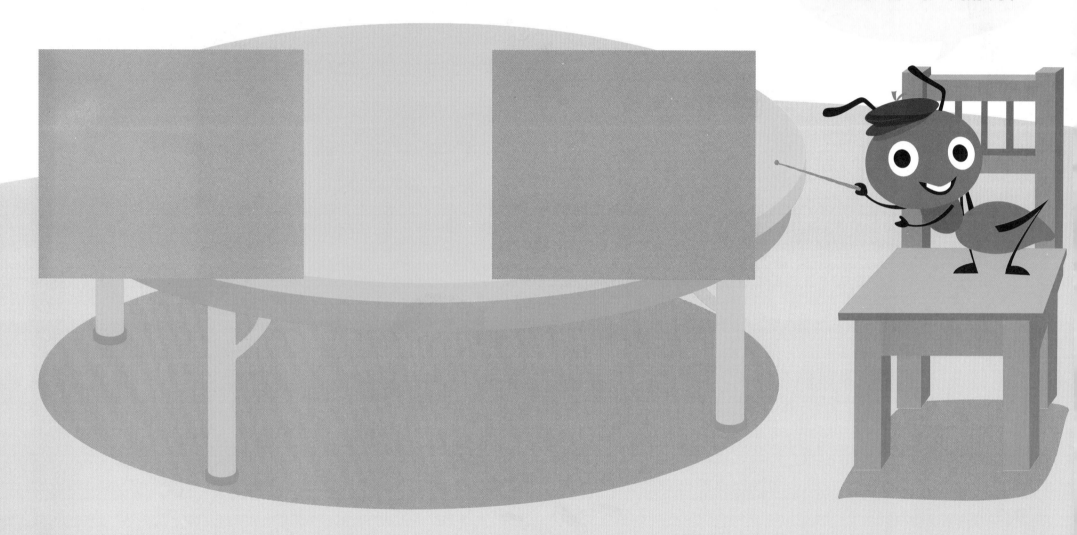

Motor Skill Practice; Visual Discrimination
Language Presentation: *This is a crayon.* Vocabulary Practice: *crayon, paper, table, chair*

5 Trace and say.

Find a chair!

Shapes: *circle*
FIND IT: *chair*

6 Color and say.

Color: *red*

Oh! It's a puppet.

School Days

What is this?

It is a puppet.

7 Draw and color yourself.

AMAZING

8 Look closely. Trace the circles.

This is my garden!

Amazing: Gardens have all kinds of living things.
Science Words: *grass, flower, ladybug*

9 **Point and say. Stick and say.**

It is a ____.

GO TO
SHOW
TIME
Page 100

MY BODY

A5 & A22

1 Look and predict.  Listen.

Find eyes!

Unit Preview; **FIND IT** in the unit: eyes

UNIT 2
13

2 Listen and say. Find and match.

Vocabulary Presentation: *eyes, nose, mouth*
Language Presentation: *What are these? They are (eyes). What is this? It is a (nose).*

A27–28

3 Listen and say. Find and match.

Vocabulary Presentation: *ears, hands, feet*; Vocabulary Practice: *eyes, nose, mouth*
Language Practice: *What are these? They are (feet).*

4 **Paste press-outs and say.**

Motor Skill Practice; Visual Discrimination
Vocabulary Presentation: *happy*, *sad*; Vocabulary Practice: *nose*, *feet*, *ears*, *eyes*, *hands*, *mouth*

5 Trace and say.

Find a crayon!

Shapes: *square*
FIND IT: *crayon*

6 Color and say.

yellow

Color: *yellow*
Review: *red*

What Is This?

 It is a face!

What is this? It is a square.

 They are circles.

 They are circles.

VALUES

Values: We greet one another.

UNIT 2

21

PROJECT **Paint a Butterfly**

9 **Point and say. Stick and say.**

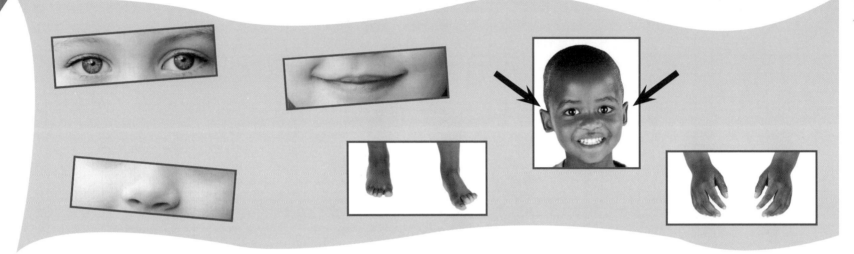

They are _____ .

GO TO
SHOW
TIME
Page 101

3 MY FAMILY

A5 & A36

'1' **Look and predict.**
Listen.

Find a baby!

Unit Preview; **FIND IT** in the unit: *baby*

A38-39

2 Listen and say. Find and match.

Vocabulary Presentation: *mother, father, baby*
Language Presentation: *Who is this? This is (my mother).*

3 Listen and say. Find and match.

Vocabulary Presentation: *brother, sister, grandparents;* Vocabulary Practice: *mother, father, baby*
Language Presentation: *Who are they? They are my grandparents.*

4 **Paste press-outs and say.**

Motor Skill Practice; Visual Discrimination
Vocabulary Practice: family members; *blue, red, yellow*

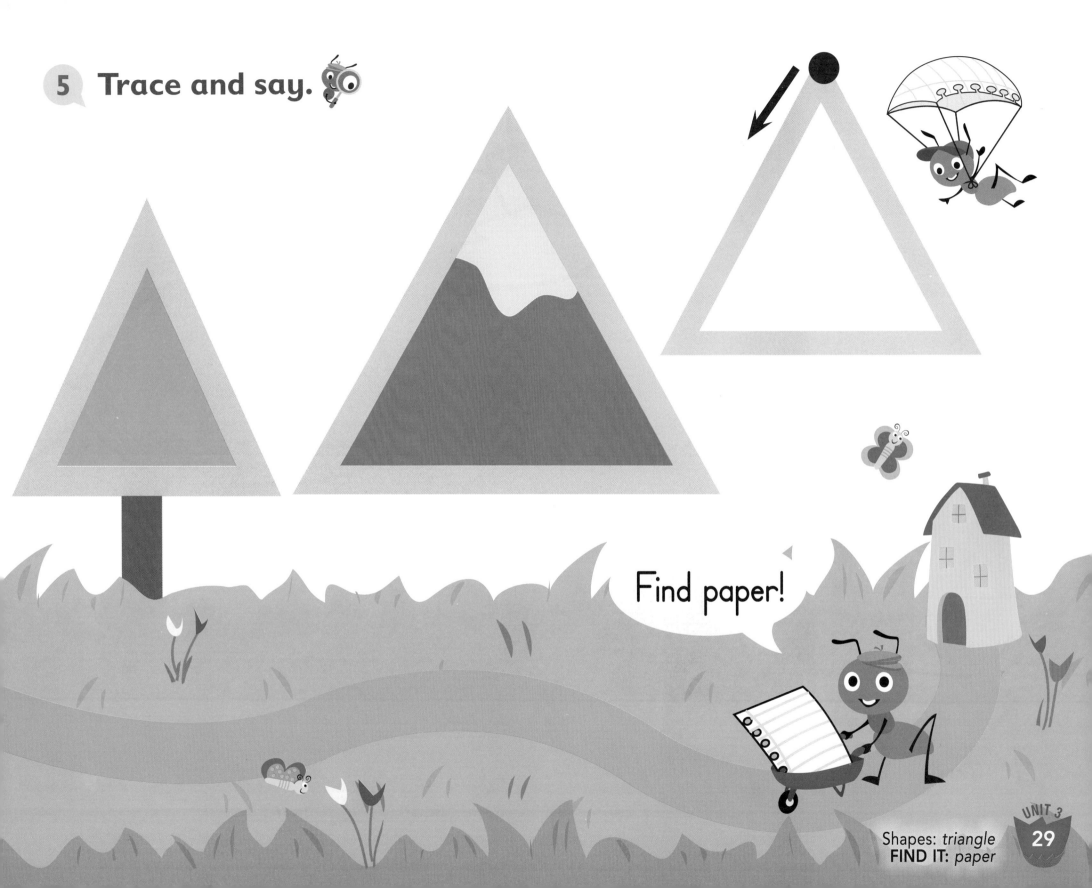

5 Trace and say.

Find paper!

Shapes: *triangle*
FIND IT: *paper*

6 **Color and say.**

Color: *blue*
Review: *red, yellow*

My Family

Hi!

This is my mother.

This is my sister. Hello!

This is my brother. What?

7 Who is respectful? Color.

Values: We respect others' things.

8 **Look closely. Trace the circles.**

This is an anthill!

Amazing: Ants live in large groups and build nests called anthills.
Science Words: *ant, anthill, family*

Make an Ant Headband

9 Point and say. Stick and say.

This is my _____ .

GO TO SHOW TIME
Page 102

MY TOYS

1 Look and predict. Listen.

Find a car!

2 Listen and say. Find and match.

Vocabulary Presentation: *doll, car, truck*
Language Presentation: *What do you want? I want (a car), please.*

3 Listen and say. Find and match.

Vocabulary Presentation: *teddy bear, airplane, ball*; Vocabulary Practice: *doll, car, truck*
Language Practice: *What do you want? I want (a ball), please.*

4 **Paste press-outs and say.**

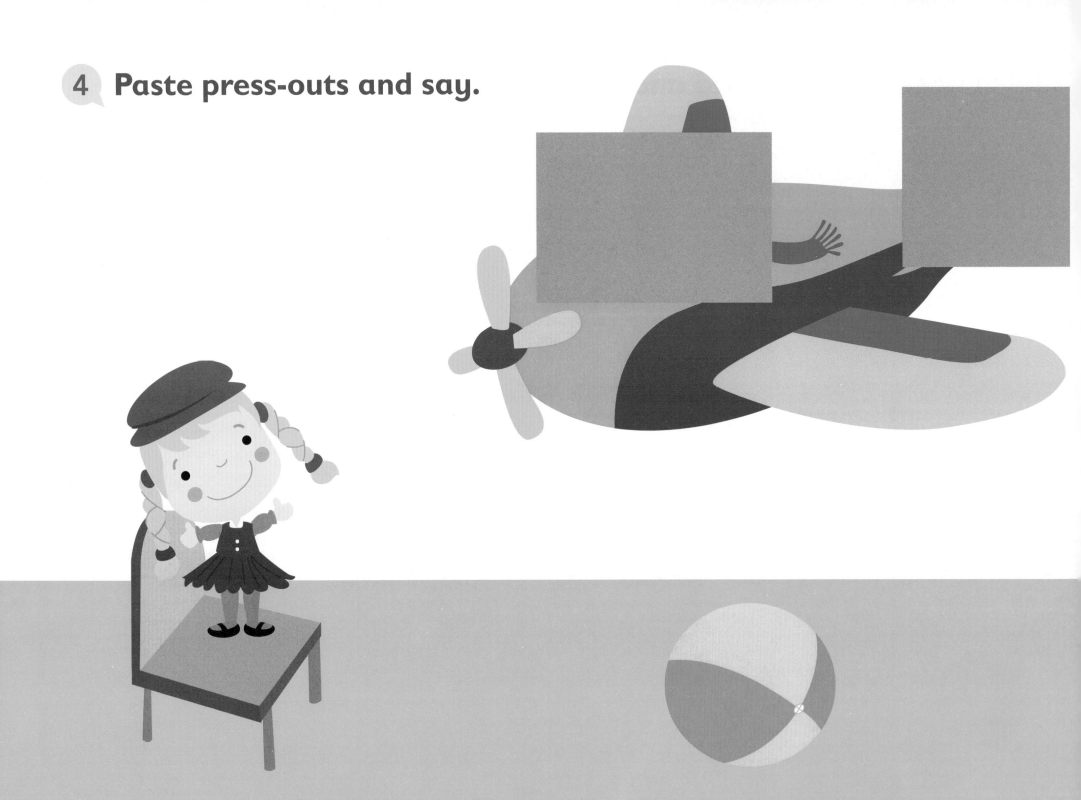

Motor Skill Practice; Visual Discrimination
Language Presentation: *in, on, under*; Vocabulary Practice: *teddy bear, airplane, doll, ball*

5 Trace and say.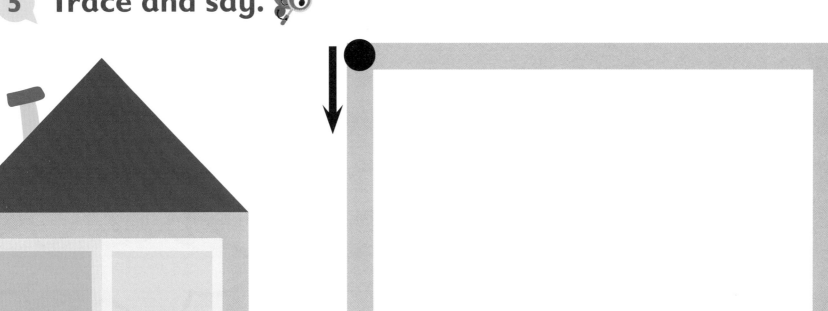

Find a doll!

6 Color and say.

green

Color: green
Review: *red, yellow, blue*

We have BIG baby dolls!

I want dolls.

Let's find dolls.

Look!

Yay!

This is the mother!

I want a doll family!

VALUES

7 Color and say.

Values: We share.
Vocabulary Practice: *doll, truck*

AMAZING

8 Look closely. Trace the circle.

I want a kite, please!

Amazing: Wind moves plants and trees.
Science Word: *wind*

PROJECT **Make a Wind Toy**

9 **Point and say. Stick and say.**

I want a [   ], please.

GO TO SHOW TIME Page 103

5 MY LUNCH

1 **Look and predict.**
Listen.

Find a cookie!

Unit Preview; **FIND IT** in the unit: *cookie*

UNIT 5
49

2 Listen and say. Find and match.

Vocabulary Presentation: *sandwich, lemonade, apple*
Language Presentation: *What do you have? I have (a sandwich).*

3 Listen and say. Find and match.

Vocabulary Presentation: *cookie, carrot, milk*; Vocabulary Practice: *sandwich, lemonade, apple*
Language Practice: *What do you have? I have (carrots).*

4 Paste press-outs and say.

Motor Skill Practice; Sequencing
Language Presentation: *Do you like (milk)? Yes./No.* Vocabulary Presentation: *bananas*; Vocabulary Practice: *milk, cookies, lemonade*

5 Find and color ●■▲■ . Say.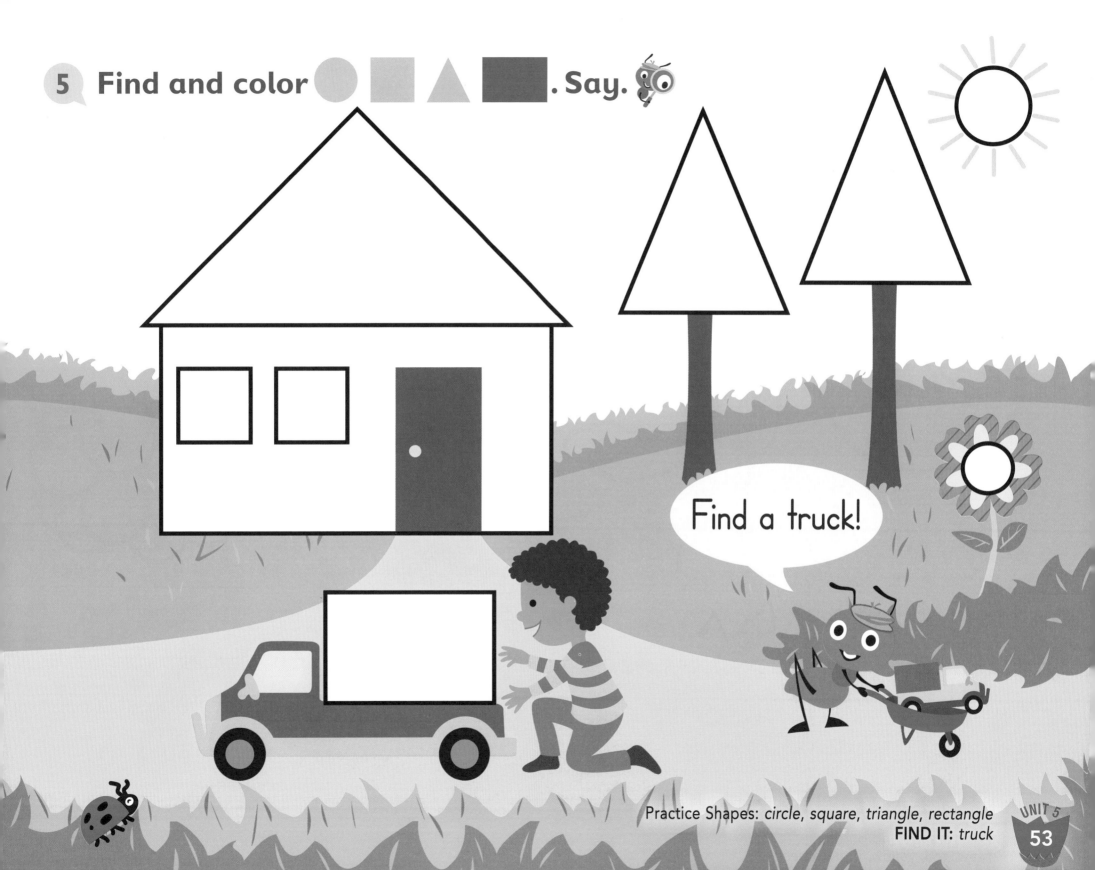

Find a truck!

Practice Shapes: *circle, square, triangle, rectangle*
FIND IT: *truck*

6 **Color and say.**

orange

purple

Colors: orange and purple
Review: red, yellow, blue, green

I ♥ you

I ♥ you

We have lunch and . . . a surprise!

I have milk.

I have carrots.

What do YOU have?

 **VALUES** **7** **Color the faces.**

Values: We try new things.

8 **Look closely. Trace the circles.**

Amazing: Some food grows on trees; other food grows in the ground.
Science Words: *lemon tree, lemon, carrot*

PROJECT

Make Lemonade

9 **Point and say. Stick and say.**

I have a ⬚ .

GO TO SHOW TIME Page 104

6 MY CLOTHES

1 Look and predict.
   Listen.

Find shoes!

Unit Preview; **FIND IT** in the unit: *shoes*

2 Listen and say. Find and match.

Vocabulary Presentation: *pants, skirt, sweater*
Language Presentation: *What do you want? I want (a skirt), please.*

3 Listen and say. Find and match.

Vocabulary Presentation: *shoes, socks, T-shirt*; Vocabulary Practice: *pants, skirt, sweater*
Language Practice: *What do you want? I want (a T-shirt), please.*

4 Paste press-outs and say.

Motor Skill Practice; Visual Discrimination
Vocabulary Presentation: *This is a (skirt). It is (purple). These are (pants). They are (blue).* Vocabulary Practice: clothing; colors

5 Trace and count. Draw 1 thing.

Find a teddy bear!

Math Presentation: *Number 1*
Vocabulary Practice: *shoe, T-shirt*; **FIND IT:** *teddy bear*

6 **Color and say.**

brown

pink

Colors: *brown* and *pink*
Review: *red, yellow, blue, green, orange, purple*

I want a picture, please!

Let's play.

Yes! Yes!

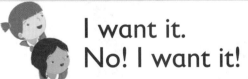 I want it.
No! I want it!

 Look at YOU!

VALUES

7 Help the boy find his shoes. Circle them.

Values: We help each other.
Vocabulary Practice: *T-shirt, pants, sweater, shoes*

UNIT 6
69

8 **Look closely. Trace the circles.**

Amazing: Rain makes animals and plants wet.
Science Words: *wet, raindrop*

PROJECT

Make Rain in a Jar

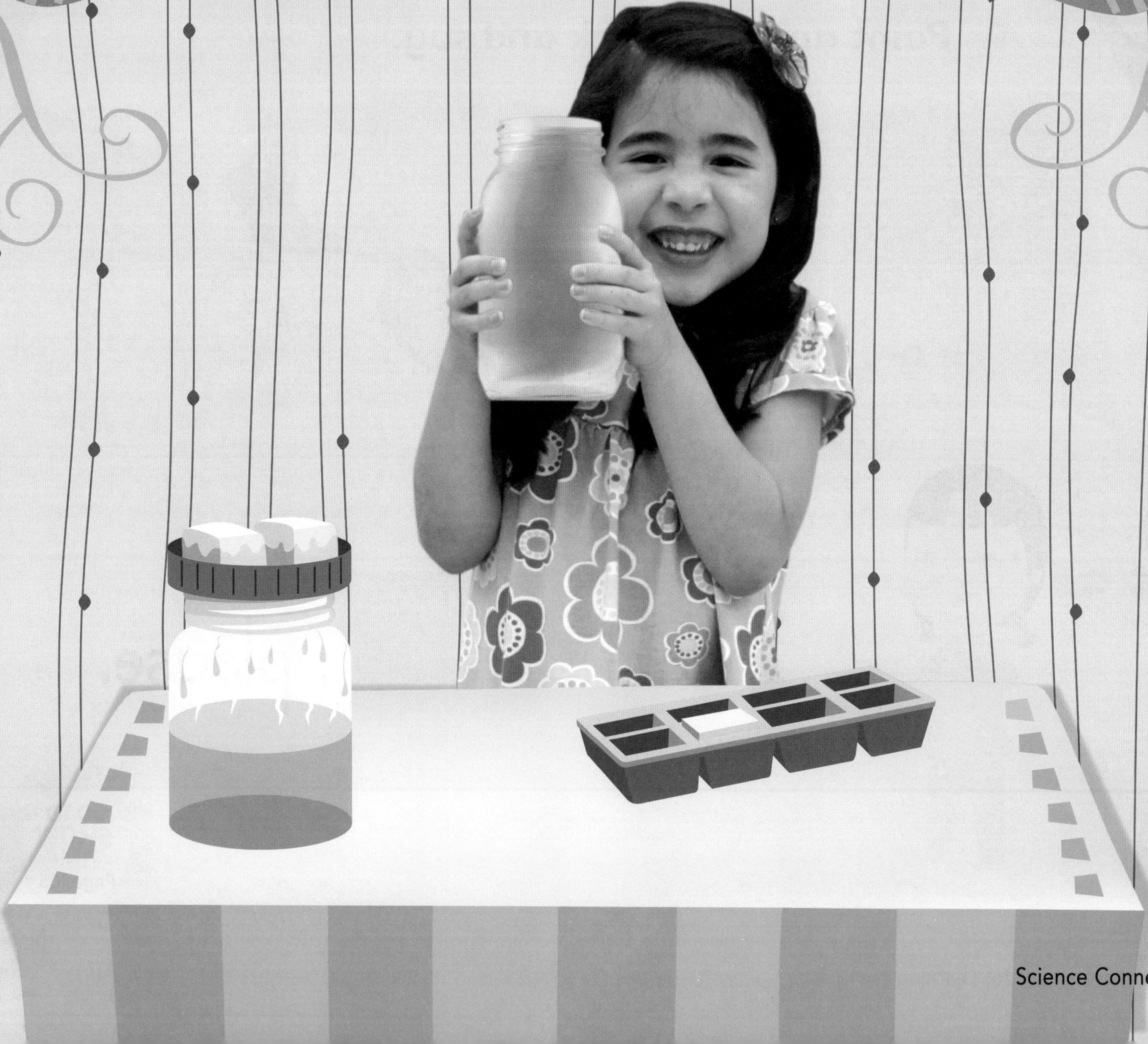

9 **Point and say. Stick and say.**

I want [ ], please.

GO TO
SHOW
TIME
Page 105

ANIMALS

A5 & B28

1 Look and predict.
Listen.

Find a fish!

Unit Preview; **FIND IT** in the unit: *fish*

2 Listen and say. Find and match.

Vocabulary Presentation: *bird, fish, cat*
Language Presentation: *What do you see? I see a (fish).*

Vocabulary Presentation: *dog, puppy, kitten*; Vocabulary Practice: *bird, fish, cat*
Language Practice: *What do you see? I see a (puppy).*

4 Paste press-outs and say.

Motor Skill Practice; Visual Discrimination
Language Presentation: *It is (big)*. Vocabulary Presentation: *big, small*; Vocabulary Practice: *dog, bird*

5 Trace and count. Draw 2 things.

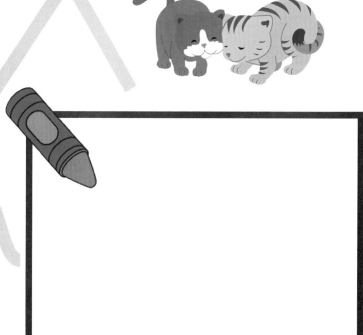

Find a ball!

Math Presentation: *Number 2*
Vocabulary Practice: *puppy, kitten*; **FIND IT:** *ball*

6 Color and say.

black

white

Colors: *black* and *white*
Review: *red, yellow, blue, green, orange, purple, brown, pink*

Where's Lucy?

I see Lucy. I see her new puppies, too!

Where's Lucy?

I don't know.

I see a crayon.

I see a fish, but where's Lucy?

VALUES

7 Trace and say.

Values: We take care of pets.
Vocabulary Practice: *fish, cat*

Amazing: A worm moves without legs or feet.
Science Words: *bug, dirt, worm*

PROJECT Make Worm Pictures

9 **Point and say. Stick and say.**

I see a ⬜.

GO TO
SHOW
TIME
Page 106

8 MY WORLD

1 Look and predict. Listen.

Find a firefighter!

2 Listen and say. Find and match.

Vocabulary Presentation: *firefighter, police officer, bus driver*
Language Presentation: *How many (firefighters) do you see? I see (two firefighters).*

3 Listen and say. Find and match.

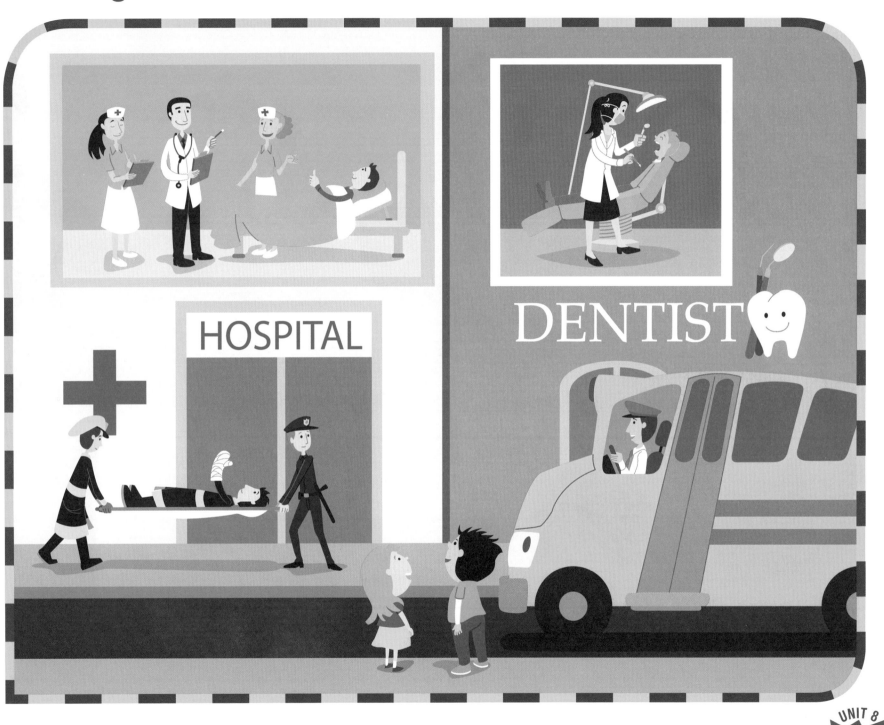

HOSPITAL

DENTIST

Vocabulary Presentation: *dentist, doctor, nurse*; Vocabulary Practice: *firefighter, police officer, bus driver*
Language Practice: *How many (doctors) do you see? I see (one doctor).*

4 Paste press-outs and say.

Motor Skill Practice; Visual Discrimination. Language Presentation: *The (nurse) has (a shot)*.
Vocabulary Presentation: *gardener, shot, baton, keys, shovel*; Vocabulary Practice: *nurse, police officer, bus driver*

5 **Trace and count. Draw 3 things.**

3

Find an apple!

Math Presentation: *Number 3*
Vocabulary Practice: *doctor, firefighter*; **FIND IT:** *apple*

6 Color and say.

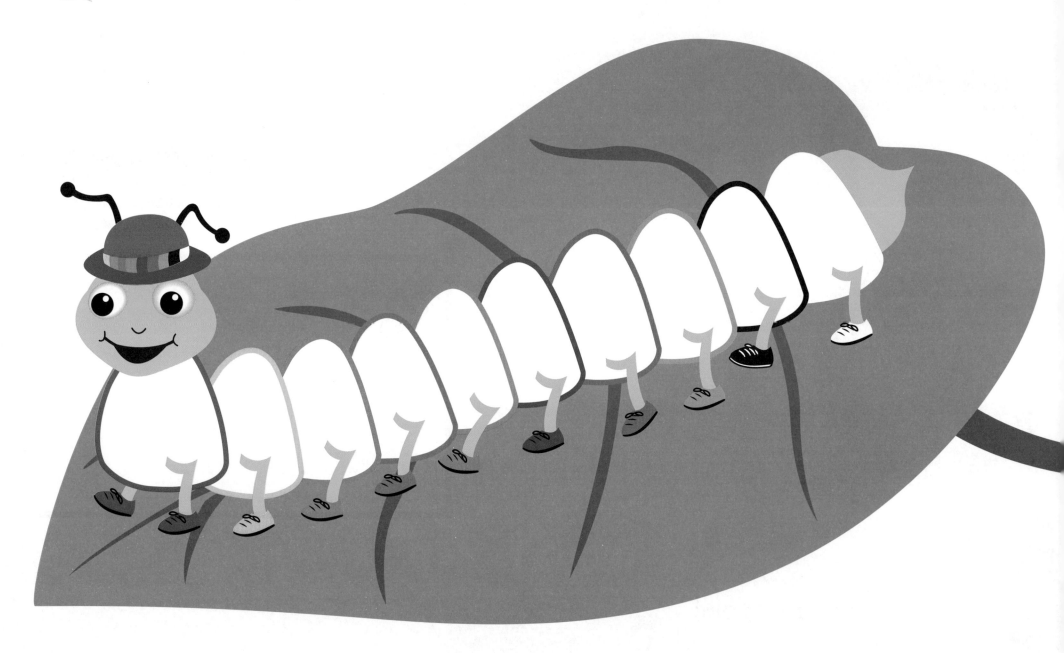

Colors Review: *red, yellow, blue, green, orange, purple, brown, pink, black, white*

Hospital

1, 2, 3.
I see 3 balloons!

I see 1 doctor.

I see 2 nurses.

I see . . .

7 Draw and color the bus.

8 Look closely. Trace the circles.

I see a flower!

Amazing: Plants and flowers grow.
Science Words: *flower, bee, grow*

PROJECT

Make Flowers

9 Point and say. Stick and say.

I see 2 _____ .

GO TO
SHOW
TIME
Page 107

9 SHOW TIME!

Listen and sing.

Find the T-shirt!

Unit Preview; **FIND IT** in the unit: *T-shirt*

Make a Mask

1.

2.

3.

Make a Puppet

1.

2.

3.

SHOW TIME

Unit 1 MY CLASS
Draw and say.

Welcome!

Unit 2 MY BODY

Draw and say.

Our Class Show

Unit 3 MY FAMILY

Draw and say.

Paint a background!

SHOW TIME

Unit 4 **MY TOYS**

Draw and say.

Have fun!

Unit 5 MY LUNCH

Draw and say.

Use props!

Unit 6 MY CLOTHES

Draw and say.

Make costumes!

Unit 7 ANIMALS

Draw and say.

Thank you!

Unit 8 MY WORLD

Draw and say.

The End

BIG FUN

1

has completed **Level 1!**

_____

Teacher